Follow Me!
Hikes for Children to Lead

Rhode Island Edition

By Kitty Opishinski

*Dedicated to Alyssa, for giving me the idea
and encouraging me to do things I love.*

ø

Cover Photo: Stone and wood face on Francis Carter Trail.
Back Cover: Lime Rock Preserve.

INTRODUCTION

This book is designed to build confidence and increase experience with leadership and problem solving, while at the same time nurturing a curiosity about and a connection to the natural world.

Many of the hikes feel remote and wild while actually having very little potential for allowing one to get truly lost. Children will have the sense of being far-removed even though they are within minutes of civilization. Hikes have been selected based on length, safety, features, and ease of navigation.

With this in mind, please let your child truly lead. Let them find the trail signs and decide which way to go. Be open to backtracking and going in circles. If they make a mistake, let them figure it out unless they are putting themselves or someone else in danger. Help if they ask but try to point them in the right direction without telling them exactly where to go.

By allowing them to 'fail softly' (without serious consequences) children learn that mistakes are part of the journey of life and often how we learn. Many important discoveries have been the results of 'failures'.

Who knows? You may discover something unexpected, too!

A NOTE TO PARENTS

♦ **LET THEM LEAD.** That's why you're here. Give your child the book and actually let *them* lead.

♦ **Allow plenty of time.** You may have to backtrack or spend time looking for the trail.

♦ **Everyone should wear appropriate shoes.** Good sturdy ones that can get wet or muddy. Nothing with open toes.

♦ **Use bug repellent and sunscreen when appropriate.**

♦ **Bring water.** Or something else that your child likes to drink.

♦ **Leave the dog at home.** You can focus on the kids and many wildlife refuges don't allow them anyway.

♦ **Check for ticks.** Take preventive measures and check everyone carefully after hiking.

♦ **Stay calm.** Take a photo of the trailmap at the trailhead if there is one. It will help you navigate and stay calm. If you are calm and enjoying yourself it's more likely your child will be able to, as well.

♦ **HAVE FUN!** Learning is important but having fun is, too, and kids learn while having fun. Try to tailor each hike to your whatever your child's interests are. If they are artistic, let them sketch, photograph or video what they see. If your child is passionate about science, take a magnifying glass. Take binoculars if your child likes nature. Let your child make the hikes their own. If they have fun, they'll want to go again.

ℒ

A NOTE TO KIDS

Your adult is letting you lead—here are a few things to remember so you might be allowed to lead again.

♦ **Walk.** A good leader stays with the group. If you don't, you are not LEADING the group, you are LEAVING the group and that's not cool. If you make the rest of the group unhappy by going too far ahead, they won't want to do this again.

♦ **Walk.** All of the trails have roots and rocks, which are great for tripping you up. If you fall and get hurt , you won't have fun and may have to leave.

♦ **Be quiet.** You will see and hear more . Most animals run and hide if they hear you coming.

♦ **Be nice to nature.** The natural world is alive. If you see any kind of animal, insect, or bird leave it alone. Stay on the trail and don't pick the flowers or break the branches. Please don't litter, either.

♦ **Stay calm.** If you get lost, don't freak out. You are not lost forever, you will be fine, and you can figure out how to get back using the directions.

♦ **Ask for help if you need it.** Making mistakes is okay. Try not to keep making the same mistake, though. That is called learning.

♦ **WALK.** (Do you get how important it is to walk yet?) It is a hike, not a race. The faster you go, the less you see and the quicker the adventure is over and you're back in the car. Why *wouldn't* you walk?

✍

RHODE ISLAND TRAILHEAD MAP

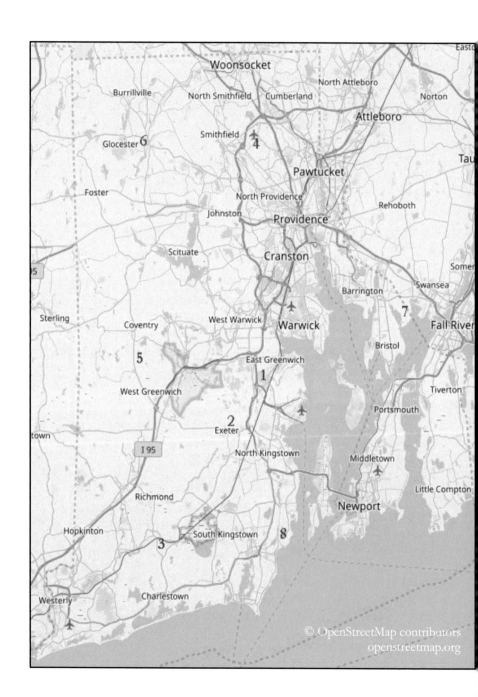

TRAILHEAD LOCATIONS

1. **Davis Memorial Wildlife Refuge:** Davisville Road, North Kingstown 02852. Trailhead is just west of 277 Davisville Road, look for sign and parking area on south side of road.

2. **Fisherville Brooks Wildlife Refuge:** 99 Pardon Joslin Road, Exeter, 02822. From Route 102, turn onto Widow Sweets Road (on the west side of the Exeter Town Clerk's Office). Take second right onto Pardon Joslin Road (a dirt road). Travel approximately one mile. Parking lot is on the right side of road by a large Fisherville Brook Wildlife Refuge sign. **Note: GPS directions are not accurate.**

3. **Francis Carter Preserve:** Use the trailhead on Carolina Back Road/Route 112 in Charlestown-NOT the Old Mill Road entrance. Trailhead located just over one mile west of junction of Route 2 and Route 112. Parking area at end of short dirt road with good signage on the road.

4. **Lime Rock Preserve:** 96 Wilbur Road, Lincoln 02865. Between Jenckes Hill Road/Route 123 and Old Louisquissett Pike/Route 246. Good signage on road.

5. **Maxwell Mays Wildlife Refuge:** 2082 Victory Highway, Coventry 02816. Large, well-marked parking area on Rt. 102 north of Meeting House Road.

6. **Sprague Farm Loop Trail:** Pine Orchard Road, Chepachet 02814. Just over two miles west of the southern intersection of Routes 102 and 44. Chestnut Hill and Pine Orchard Road are the same road.

7. **Touisset Marsh Wildlife Refuge:** 99 Touisset Road, Warren 02885. Trailhead is behind the parking lot of the Fire Department located at the corner where Touisset Road becomes Maple Road. Park in the firehouse lot to the right of the building where ample space is provided.

8. **Whale Rock Trail:** One mile north of Narragansett Beach, on Route 1A/Boston Neck Road is Sprague Bridge. On the north side of the bridge, Old Boston Neck Road runs off to the east. The trailhead is located at the corner where Old Boston Neck Road takes a ninety degree turn. Drive through the hedge of trees to a small well-marked parking area.

✍

Note: Use of the information in this book is at the sole risk of the user.

1. Davis Memorial Wildlife Refuge   .75 mi/Easy

♦ You can go to RIGHT or LEFT when you start—it's a loop.
♦ Follow the Orange Trail markers.
♦ Watch for the huge electrical poles—they are halfway through.
♦ Walk past the poles just a bit and turn around to see the sign showing you where the trail goes.
♦ DO NOT WALK ALONG UNDER THE ELECTRICAL WIRES. This will take you away from the trail. (Notice there are no Orange Trail makers under the wires.)

Top-Species Identification Board (l) and log steps (r).
Bottom-Orange Trail marker (circled, l) and mossy log (r).

What You Might See:

☐ Massive Poles

☐ Birds

☐ Water

☐ Fenced Cemetery

☐ Square Granite Property Marker

☐ Animals

☐ Fallen Trees

☐ Moth Traps

What You Might Hear:

☐ Traffic

☐ Birds

☐ Wildlife

What You Might Smell:

☐ Earth

☐ Pine

What You Might Touch:

☐ Moss

☐ Wood

☐ Leaves

☐ Metal

Top-Photo of trail map at the trailhead.

Bottom-Electrical poles (l) and trail direction sign (circled, r) at base of poles.

What season is it:

What did you see:

What did you hear:

What's the weather:

What did you touch:

What did you smell:

2. Fisherville Brooks Wildlife Refuge   1.3 mi/Easy

- Take the Blue Trail starting next to the sign in the parking lot. It's a loop but to follow these directions, go RIGHT to start the trail. Other trails connect to the Blue Trail so watch your signs carefully.
- At first trail split, go STRAIGHT on the Blue Trail. The Yellow trail goes off to the right.
- Go STRAIGHT at next split. The Yellow trail re-connects here.
- At next split, turn LEFT. The Blue and Orange Trails run along together here and this should take you back to the parking lot.

Top-Blue Trail marker (circled, l) and trail split sign by bench (r).

Bottom-Beaver lodge (l) and tree chewed by beavers (r).

What You Might See:

- ☐ Bridges
- ☐ Boardwalk
- ☐ Bench
- ☐ Birdhouses
- ☐ Beaver Dam
- ☐ Dam and waterfall
- ☐ Birds
- ☐ Animals
- ☐ Fallen Trees
- ☐ A long rock that sticks out of the ground like a dinosaur's back

What You Might Hear:

- ☐ Water
- ☐ Birds
- ☐ Wildlife

What You Might Smell:

- ☐ Earth
- ☐ Pine

What You Might Touch:

- ☐ Moss
- ☐ Wood
- ☐ Earth
- ☐ Water

Top-Bridge over dam.

Bottom-Footbridge over stream (l) and a rustic shelter (r).

What season is it:

What did you see:

What did you hear:

What's the weather:

What did you touch:

What did you smell:

3. Francis Carter Preserve   1.5 mi./Medium

This trail is a one-and-a-half mile loop that has a big, old stone dam about half the way through. It also has the rock that is in the picture on the cover—see if you can find it! There are a lot of different trails, though, so follow directions carefully.

♦ Go STRAIGHT at the first set of trail signs. You are taking the Moraine Loop and you need to follow the Split Rock Loop (marked with white squares) to get to it. You should see the tree identification sign (below) very soon.

♦ At the second sign go RIGHT to start on the Moraine Loop, marked with orange squares.

♦ When the Orange and Blue Trail (which is the Old Pasture Loop) connect, go LEFT. The trails are together so you should see orange and blue trail markers.

♦ When they split, go LEFT again. You should be on the trail marked with orange again.

♦ Where the white trail connects, go to the LEFT (more like straight). The white and orange trails are together here for a short time.

♦ When you get to the set of trail signs you saw when you started, go RIGHT to get back to the parking lot.

Tree identification sign (l) and sign overlooking vernal pool (r).

What You Might See:

☐ Signs

☐ A Bench

☐ Water

☐ Big Rocks

☐ A Dam

☐ Animals

☐ Fallen Trees

☐ An observation deck

What You Might Hear:

☐ Airplanes

☐ Birds

☐ Wildlife

What You Might Smell:

☐ Earth

☐ Pine

☐ Mud

What You Might Touch:

☐ Moss   ☐ Wood   ☐ Leaves   ☐ Rocks

Top-Woodpecker holes on a dead tree (l) and Orange Trail marker (circled, r).
Bottom-Photo of trail map sign at trailhead (l) and a bench on the trail (r).

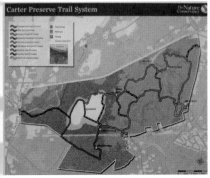 

What season is it:

What did you see:

What did you hear:

What's the weather:

What did you touch:

What did you smell:

4. Lime Rock Preserve   2 mi./Medium

This trail starts out along an old electric trolley line so the trail is raised up above the ground on the sides to start. In this area, the marble ledges make a special kind of soil where over 30 rare plant species grow. That is more than any other Nature Conservancy site in Rhode Island! After you turn off the raised section, the trail loops around and across the top of the dirt dam at one end of the Manton Reservoir.

♦ Follow trail marked with yellow rectangles the whole way.
♦ After passing the ravine on the left, watch for trail to go to RIGHT. If you get to the huge pile of rocks, you missed the turn. Go back a little bit and watch for the trail to go to LEFT now.
♦ Where the blue trail connects, marked with blue and yellow rectangles, go STRAIGHT.
♦ At the next split, go LEFT to get back to parking lot.

The trail on the old trolley line (l) and a stream running off of the Manton Reservoir (r).

What You Might See:

☐ Birds

☐ People

☐ Water

☐ Animals

What You Might Hear:

☐ Airplanes

☐ Birds

☐ People

What You Might Smell:

☐ Mud

☐ Flowers

☐ Wood Smoke

☐ Pine

What You Might Touch:

☐ Rocks

☐ Wood

☐ Leaves

☐ Water

Top: Signs at the trailhead (l) and a common painted turtle (r).

Bottom: Stairs on the trail (l) and trail across the top of the earth dam (r).

What season is it:

What did you see:

What did you hear:

What's the weather:

What did you touch:

What did you smell:

5. Maxwell Mays Wildlife Refuge   1.3 mi/Moderate

Look for an old stone chimney as you hike—no one knows what it is from or who built it. There are sometimes otters and beavers in the pond so watch for those too! You might see some private homes on this hike so make sure you stay on the trail and don't go into someone's yard.

♦ The trailhead is across the parking lot from the signs/map.

♦ Follow the signs that say TRAILS next to the trees. There will be a field on your right. Keep following the signs to a second field.

♦ In the second field watch for a break in the stone wall on your left. It is marked with a sign for the Carr Pond (CP) trail, marked with white rectangles. Go LEFT through the wall here. Directly ahead, at the corner of the field, you will see a sign that says TRAILS and has an arrow that points to the right. **Ignore that sign.**

♦ At the first split, go RIGHT. The Hammett Hill trail, marked with yellow rectangles, goes off to the left here.

♦ At the next split, go RIGHT again. This is where the Yellow Trail re-connects to the White Trail.

♦ Follow the sign that says PARKING to go across the dirt road. At the corner of the field go RIGHT and follow the path. This is the end of the loop. Keep following the signs to the parking lot.

> **BONUS:** *This property was once owned by the artist, Maxwell Mays. He gave the land to the Audubon Society and they manage it now. There are seven marked sites that have activities to go with them. They can be found at the Audubon Society of Rhode Island's Maxwell Mays website.*

Trail direction sign/trail maps at trailhead (l) and the trail winding through huge rocks (r).

What You Might See:

- Signs
- Houses
- Water
- Big Rocks
- An Old Stone Chimney
- Animals
- Fallen Trees
- Stone Walls

What You Might Hear:

- Airplanes
- Birds
- Wildlife

What You Might Smell:

- Earth
- Pine
- Mud

What You Might Touch:

- Wood
- Rocks
- Moss
- Earth
- Water

Top: Sign at the trailhead about the man who used to own the property.

Bottom: Old stone chimney (l) and a male mallard duck (r).

25

What season is it:

What did you see:

What did you hear:

What's the weather:

What did you touch:

What did you smell:

6. Sprague Farm Town Loop   3.8mi/Hard

This is the most challenging hike in the book because it is long and you change trails twice. Make sure you have plenty of time and be sure to watch for the trail signs.

♦ Go LEFT from the parking lot on the Sprague Trail, marked with white rectangles.
♦ At the end, go RIGHT on the Haystack Hill Trail, marked with yellow rectangles. Follow trail marked with yellow rectangles on Haystack Hill Trail.
♦ This connects with the Colonel Anthony Trail, marked with orange dots. Go RIGHT. Follow trail marked with orange dots on Colonel Anthony Trail.
♦ When this connects to the Sprague Trail, marked with white rectangles, go LEFT to get back to the parking lot.

Top: White Trail marker (circled, l) and information board with trail map at trailhead (r).

Bottom: Sunken foundation (l) and a wild turkey (r).

What You Might See:

- ☐ Signs
- ☐ Birds
- ☐ Water
- ☐ Sunken Building Foundations
- ☐ Stone Walls
- ☐ Fallen Trees
- ☐ Animals
- ☐ Big Cement Circles

What You Might Hear:

- ☐ Airplanes
- ☐ Birds
- ☐ Wildlife

What You Might Smell:

- ☐ Earth
- ☐ Pine

What You Might Touch:

- ☐ Stone
- ☐ Wood
- ☐ Moss
- ☐ Metal
- ☐ Soil

Top: Trail direction signs.

Bottom: A tunnel of trees (l) and one of the many signs on the property (r).

George & Sarah A. Sprague Farmstead

This site is their farmstead which includes the house and barn foundations. George died in 1879 at the age of 90 years and his wife Sarah, commonly known as Sally Ann, died six years later in 1885 at the age of 86 years. George and Sarah had at least two and possibly as many as five children. None of the children outlived their parents. George was 33 and Sarah was 23 when Amanda was born in 1822. Amanda lived until 1873 when she died at the age of 51 and does not appear to have ever married. Amanda had a younger sister, Junealta, who was born in 1831 but only lived until she was 8 years old. Perhaps Amanda decided not to get married and move away, but as the only living offspring she chose to stay on the farm to help her parents as they grew old. Or perhaps Amanda had a disability that kept her on this farm under her parents care. We simply do not know, we can only imagine.

Fieldstone grave markers in the family cemetery suggest that three other children were born to George and Sarah, but none lived beyond infancy. All are buried on the family cemetery which is on this land trust property and has been lovingly restored.

George was the third generation of Sprague's to farm this land. His brother Smith Sprague has a farmstead further down this trail.

29

What season is it:

What did you see:

What did you hear:

What's the weather:

What did you touch:

What did you smell:

7. <u>Touisset Marsh Wildlife Refuge</u> 2mi/Moderate

This trail is not marked as clearly as the others in the book but it is a loop. There are trails that cut across the loop but if you follow directions, you will wind up back at the parking area.

♦ Go LEFT out of the parking area—not down the path with the big metal gate. There should be a field on your left and trees on your right.

♦ Stay on the path next to the trees. Watch for it to cut through the trees, and go to the RIGHT here. This takes you to another field.

♦ In this field, go LEFT and stay next to the trees again.

♦ At the other end of the second field, the trail goes LEFT through the trees to a third field.

♦ Stay on the trail with the trees on your right until the other end of the field. Watch for the trail to go back into the trees and turn RIGHT.

♦ Just after this you should come to a bridge.

♦ At every trail crossing after this, go STRAIGHT OR LEFT (if there is no straight) and you will wind up back at the parking lot. The last thing you will see is the big metal gate mentioned above.

Trailhead sign (l) and photo of trail map at the trailhead (r).

What You Might See:

- [ ] Signs
- [ ] A Bench
- [ ] Water
- [ ] A Boardwalk
- [ ] Bluebird boxes
- [ ] Animals
- [ ] A bridge
- [ ] Buildings

What You Might Hear:

- [ ] Airplanes
- [ ] Birds
- [ ] Water
- [ ] People
- [ ] Wind
- [ ] Boats

What You Might Smell:

- [ ] Earth
- [ ] Pine
- [ ] Mud

What You Might Touch:

- [ ] Wood
- [ ] Rocks
- [ ] Mud
- [ ] Metal

Top: A section of boardwalk.

Bottom: A small crab, the picture makes it look bigger than it really is, (l) and the bridge (r).

What season is it:

What did you see:

What did you hear:

What's the weather:

What did you touch:

What did you smell:

8. Whale Rock Trail
1.7 mi/Easy

- There is a field with bluebird boxes next to the parking area. Stay away from the boxes-don't disturb them or the birds.
- Walk down dirt road on left side of parking area to the trailhead.
- There is a house on the right. Stay out of their yard.
- This is a straight in-and-out trail with some boardwalks but no trail signs to watch for.
- There is a rocky beach at the end of the trail.

Top: View of Whale Rock (circled) at the end of the trail.

Bottom: Parking area and dirt road to trailhead (l) and a section of boardwalk (r).

What You Might See:

☐ Water

☐ A Boardwalk

☐ An Island

☐ Birdhouses

☐ A Fence

☐ Boats

☐ Birds

☐ Animals

☐ Fallen Trees

☐ Big Rocks

What You Might Hear:

☐ Water

☐ Bird

☐ Boats

What You Might Smell:

☐ Earth

☐ The Ocean

☐ Pine

What You Might Touch:

☐ Wood

☐ Water

☐ Rocks

☐ Metal

☐ Sand

Top: The trailhead sign.

Bottom: The beach at the end (l) and a tree on the trail (r).

What season is it:

What did you see:

What did you hear:

What's the weather:

What did you touch:

What did you smell:

THANKS

I would like to thank my husband, Tom, and daughters, Alyssa, Ana, and Laura, for their unwavering support, willingness to walk many miles, and constant help on so many fronts. My sister, Gail, also deserves recognition for proofreading, editing, and formatting suggestions and for being such a great sister. To the many families who agreed to be guinea pigs and let their children lead them with potentially incorrect directions, I salute your bravery and patience. You helped bring this book into being. Thank you all.

AFTERWORD

Try to re-hike the same trail at different times of the year. Each season offers new discoveries and a trail changes dramatically as the year passes. You should become more comfortable as the hikes become familiar. Look for changes in the trail each time you're out and use the book to write down what you see.

Do you have a favorite trail that you'd like to share? A correction, compliment or concern about the book? Please email **followme.hikesforkids@gmail.com**

AUTHOR'S INFO

Kitty Opishinski, BA English, is a wife and the mother of three successful grown daughters. She has lived in Rhode Island for over 30 years and often refers to it as the condensed soup of states (a compliment). She still enjoys discovering new things in the area.

Before moving to Rhode Island, Kitty grew up in Key Largo, Florida. She was fortunate to have an excellent Girl Scout leader when she was a girl and to later be a leader herself. She attributes much of her love of nature to these influences.

Made in the USA
Middletown, DE
27 July 2020